PRACTICAL BLOGGING FOR EVERYBODY

ANTHONY EKANEM

ISBN 979-888521413-1

Dedicated to my family and the readers.

Contents

Preface

Blogs are everywhere. Despite this, people seem to have stopped talking about them as a way of making money online. Well, in my opinion, blogs are still very much an essential part of a successful online business. A blog can make you money, build a relationship with your subscribers and generate traffic to your website. Yes, everyone's talking about Facebook, Twitter, and Google+ – and on the surface of it, blogging may today appear a little 'old hat' – but that doesn't mean you should leave blogging on the table.

Not only is blogging good for business, but it is also fun and can help you to build relationships with other marketers. This could lead to Joint Venture deals and collaborations etc. – and it's a bonus of blogging that often gets overlooked.

Look at the top internet marketers. They all have a blog. There's also niche blogging – and it's certainly a very valid way of making money online, especially if you can build up a large portfolio of blogs in different niches.

In this book, I'm going to show you how to set up and run a successful blog. We'll discuss the techy side of installing a blog, filling it with content, monetizing it and driving traffic to it. We'll also discuss things such as how a blog can help you to build a list and how you can 'flip' blogs for profit.

Whether you want to become a niche blogger – or you're looking at running a personal blog or a blog for your business – I hope that this guide will help.

Acknowledgements

I hereby acknowledge all who inspired the writing of this book.

CHAPTER ONE

Choosing a Blogging Platform

When starting a blog, you have many options. As with most things in life, there isn't a right or a wrong solution. Each option has some major advantages and disadvantages, which we're going to now talk about.

Blogger.com

Blogger.com provides possibly the easiest way to start a blog. Unlike other blogging platforms which require you to have webspace and install blogging software, with Blogger you simply visit the website, create an account – and then build your blog using a point and click web interface. It's very simple and best of all free. You don't even need to have a domain name or web hosting. You can have a blog online in around fifteen minutes – and they also provide themes and layouts so that you can customize your blog and make it look a particular way.

Blogger.com certainly has its advantages and it can sometimes be a good solution. If you feel uncomfortable with setting up a hosting account and want to get a new blog online as quickly as possible then it can provide a decent solution. So, why is it then that it isn't recommended? There are several major drawbacks to

Blogger, one of which can be serious and might not rear its ugly head until several years down the line.

One of the main problems is that you never actually own your blog. Blogger.com is owned by Google and essentially all you are doing is borrowing their website to host your blog. You are bound by their rules and decisions – and thus they can come along at any time and shut down your blog. If you've spent two years building your blog and writing posts then it's just too bad. You will lose it all – and there generally isn't a lot you can do about it.

You might think "well, I'm running a legitimate blog, they're never going to shut down my site" – but this isn't necessarily so. I have seen cases of successful, popular, and legitimate blogs being shut down for seemingly no reason. I'm sure there was a reason, of course, it just seems that way. But that's not the only issue.

One of the biggest problems with Blogger is that it's inflexible. Sure, they provide you with some templates, layouts, and widgets to choose from – but there is nothing like the range available for other blogging platforms such as WordPress.

Squarespace

Squarespace is an increasingly popular blogging platform and is worthy of your consideration. Unlike Blogger or WordPress (covered next), Squarespace isn't free and attracts a membership fee.

They host the whole thing (so it could still potentially be vulnerable to deletion, although I'm told this isn't a problem on SquareSpace. Important: You would need to look into that yourself though!)

At the time of writing, prices start at $12 a month for a 20-page website and 3GB storage. The site is extremely easy to use and has the benefit of being customisable. Where

Squarespace excels though is in security. There is generally a much lesser risk of your blog being hacked when compared to other open-source platforms such as WordPress.

You might like this added security, the ease of use and the backup support provided. You may however be turned off by the price. So, Squarespace is a good solution, but it remains a relatively small niche player when compared to the daddy of them all – WordPress.

WordPress

WordPress is probably the most popular blogging platform and it's the one most people use – so this is the one we're going to concentrate on primarily during this report. You can see an example of a WordPress blog in the screenshot below:

Why is WordPress so great?

It's extremely user friendly, you own your blog (unlike Blogger where it can be deleted by someone else) and it's extremely customizable. With a WordPress site, you can do anything with it. From a simple blog, right through to a complex e-commerce store incorporating many features, WordPress can usually be adapted to suit what you require. There are thousands of different templates to choose from. Some are free and some are paid – but there is nearly always something which suits your needs.

There are also thousands of widgets and add-ons which can be added to your blog to improve functionality and even make you money. As with anything, WordPress isn't perfect though.

WordPress is often said to be vulnerable to being hacked. I've had it happen myself and it's something you need to take seriously. To minimize the risk, make sure that you regularly back up your site and install the latest updates when they come out. WordPress is always being updated, with bugs and security hole fixes. Don't let that put you off though. I'm a huge fan of WordPress and (in my opinion at least) it remains the best solution.

CHAPTER TWO

Setting Up Your WordPress Blog

First, you'll require a web hosting account and a domain name for your blog (a .com is ideal because it appeals to people across the globe). Web hosting can be bought very cheaply from various companies – but try and get one that uses C-Panel. This makes setting things up much easier.

Although it is by no means the only provider, I recommend Hostgator as I have always been satisfied with the service and if there is a problem their support is usually pretty good. Domain names can also be bought from various providers but the one I usually use is called Namecheap. Once you've registered your domain name for your blog, and have sorted out a hosting account, follow the instructions below. I have assumed that you are using Hostgator and Namecheap, but the process should be similar even if you are using different providers.

Before we begin, I just want to add that you shouldn't be put off even if you don't consider yourself a 'techy' person. Installing WordPress is easy and once you've done it the first time it will be even easier next time.

a. The first step is to do set up the name servers so that they point to your hosting account. Visit http://www.namecheap.com, login, and you will be taken to the page below. Click on 'view':

b. Choose the domain name that you want to set name servers for and click on 'Edit Selected':

c. Click on 'Transfer DNS to Webhost' from the list on the left sidebar:

d. On the form that appears, type in the DNS of your web hosting provider into fields 1 and 2. Your hosting provider will give you these details. If you're not sure, give them a call and they will be able to tell you the addresses – or at least point you to where you can find them. Alternatively, look through the help section in your hosting account – they will probably be there. Once you have done that click on 'Save Changes.'

Now we need to log in to our hosting account or 'C Panel'. Log in with your hosting account's username and password, and then once you are there scroll down to where it says Domains, and click on 'Addon Domains.'

Fill in the New Domain Name, and the next two entries will be automatically entered for you.

I usually like to let the system generate a random password for me, so it's nice and secure. Write down the password as you'll need it later, then click on 'Add Domain.'

Now we are ready to install WordPress!

- So back on the main home page of the control panel, we will have to scroll down to almost the bottom to find the

Fantastico De Luxe button:

- Select WordPress from the list that appears:
- Select New Installation

Where it says 'install on domain' choose the domain you registered from the drop-down box. You don't need to enter anything in the 'install in directory.'

Choose a new username and password, which you will use to log in and post content on your blog. In the base configuration, choose the name you will post as, email address, site name, and description. In the site name and description, try to use some of those keywords for SEO purposes. Then click on 'Install WordPress.'

On the next screen click on 'Finish Installation' to complete the install of WordPress!

Check your installation worked correctly by going to your domain name.

CHAPTER THREE

Essential Tweaks to Your Blog

Your basic blog should now be installed – but as you can see it currently looks boring. What we want to do is spice up the design a little and add some essential plugins and other tweaks. Let's tackle the design first and choose a WordPress theme.

WordPress blogs use themes that change the design of your blog. Now you have a couple of main options here. You can either get someone to design you a custom, unique theme – or you could use one of the thousands of ready-made themes which are available online.

The former is more expensive, but you have the advantage that your blog will be 100% unique. If you know where to look it's also possible to find people who will do it at a reasonable cost. So, getting a custom-made blog theme designed is an option that is seriously worth considering – but even so most people will go for the option of downloading a ready-made WordPress theme.

There are thousands of different themes available – and some are paid, whilst some are free. In general, it's often better to go for a paid theme. They are usually available cheaply and you will find that they are not as common as the free ones.

Do you want a blog that looks like thousands of other people? Probably not – and by investing a little in a paid theme you also usually get something that looks more professional and can be more easily customized.

There is no shortage of companies and websites offering WordPress themes. There is an almost mind-boggling range of different options.

Some things to think about when choosing a theme... There is no 'right or wrong' or 'best' theme. The theme you choose will depend on your needs, what you intend to use the blog for and how much you're willing to spend. Even so, there are some things to bear in mind:

How common is the theme? Some themes are very common indeed and you'll see them being used on different sites across the internet. In general, it's best to use a theme that isn't as common, so it's a good idea to look at how many times the theme has been downloaded – or do a quick Google search for the theme name and see if you can find other blogs that are also using it.

What is the subject/niche of your blog – and what do you intend to use it for? You'll often find that certain themes are aimed at specific subjects, niches, or types of users. For example, if you're a photographer particular themes are laid out in a way that makes it easy to present your portfolio. Similarly, some themes are aimed at e-commerce users or types of bloggers. It might just come down to your niche - if you're going to be blogging about golf, for example, choose a theme that incorporates a golf design etc.

What layout do you want? The layout of your blog is very important and different themes use different layouts. Some are one column, some are two, some are three columns etc. Increasingly many themes incorporate a degree of flexibility and let you choose how many columns etc.; you want for certain pages – but have a long hard think about what layout would suit your blog best. You might, for example, decide that three columns would work best – one for a side menu, another for the actual blog posts and another for adverts – or you might decide you would prefer a blog with a top menu and therefore prefer a two-column layout.

Consider the theme options and features. Whilst the look and feel of the blog design is important, don't forget about the admin system and features that sits behind the theme. A good blog theme will be easily customized and support different features. Look out for a theme that fully supports the latest version of WordPress and which is widget-ready. Thoroughly research which parts of the theme can be customized (e.g., the header, footer, theme colours etc.) and how easy this is to do.

Go for function over form. This is a continuation of the last point. Choose a theme that has the layout and functionality you are looking for over a theme that looks good but is the wrong layout and/or doesn't have the features you require. If you choose a theme that has the correct layout and features, and it comes with functionality that makes it easily customized then it should be easy to create the blog you want.

Do your research and have a look around at the different themes available. If you spend an hour or two just browsing, you should come across a few themes that catch your eye and you will begin to get a feel for the features different themes offer. Look at the reviews for each theme too – you will get a good idea of how satisfied people are with it.

Once you have created a shortlist of possible themes you can then compare them next to each other and choose your favourite. Once you have downloaded the theme to your computer, installing it on your blog is usually just as simple as uploading it into the blog folder using your FTP program and then activating it by logging into your WP-Admin area

Tweak Your Theme

Once you've got your blog theme installed, most people are going to want to tweak it a little. This might just be as simple as replacing the default images with those of your own (you just replace the original image files using your FTP program)

Install Some Essential Plugins

One of the great things about WordPress is the thousands of plugins that are available. So, it makes sense to begin by installing some of the essential ones.

Akismet

Nearly every WordPress blog has Akismet installed – and it is one of the first plugins you should install on your blog. In a nutshell, Akismet helps to stop spam comments on your blog and saves you the hassle of manually deleting them all. Spam is a real problem on blogs – and whilst this plugin doesn't eradicate the problem it is generally effective.

Online Backup for WordPress

A lot of work will go into your blog – so imagine waking up one day and losing it all – or accidentally deleting something crucial and finding your blog doesn't work anymore! It's not something you want to happen to you, so it makes sense to back up your blog regularly – and this little plugin makes it easy to do so.

Google XML Sitemaps

This plugin builds a sitemap of your blog and then submits it to Google. Quite simply a site map is a list or directory of all the pages and posts on your blog – and it makes it easier for search engines such as Google to crawl the pages and index your site faster.

All In One SEO Pack

This is a great tool for your blog. It allows you to customize the meta tags for each blog post, so you can optimize them for their keywords.

Aweber Web Form Plugin

Your blog is a great way to build a list. If you use Aweber (one of the most popular providers of email marketing solutions) then the above plugin makes it easy to install an opt-in box onto your blog.

Mobile Apps

Ok – this one isn't a plugin – but it is an essential download if you own a smartphone such as an iPhone or a Blackberry.

With the range of WordPress mobile apps you can make posts to your site whilst on the go, which is something I find particularly useful:

CHAPTER FOUR

Filling Your Blog with Contents

This is where blogging starts – making blog posts! So, by now, you should have a nice pretty blog, but the reason people will come to your blog is the content. It's at the heart of any blog - and without good blog posts, a blog isn't a blog!

How do you create content? Well, there are several options. Ultimately you can create it yourself, use and adapt ready-made content – or outsource it. The one you choose will largely depend on your time, ability, budget – and what sort of blog it is. If it's a niche blog, you should seriously consider outsourcing your blog posts or adapting private label rights material.

If it's a personal blog, you would probably be best at writing the content yourself. After all, nobody else can really "be" you. Ok, let's take you through each option and discuss some of the main pros and cons of each.

Autoblog Content

Autoblogs are a popular solution for niche blogs. As the name suggests, an autoblog is a blog where the content is posted automatically via a plugin that sources articles from the internet and posts them to your blog on autopilot.

The beauty of this of course is that it makes everything extremely easy. It's largely a setup-and-leave solution – and thus it can take away a lot of the stress usually associated with running a blog.

But while it seems like a good solution on the surface, auto blog content is full of problems and as such is not recommended for most blogs. The obvious disadvantage is that none of the content on your blog will be yours. It will be full of duplicate content – and some of it may not be what you want to appear on your blog.

Look at a typical auto blog and it's usually obvious to even the most casual user that the blog has simply been set up to make money. It's not a "real" blog written by a real person – and as such people are unlikely to take it very seriously.

Use PLR

Another relatively easy way of filling your blog with content is to use Private Label Rights (PLR) articles. PLR is readily available online and gives you pre-written content on a specific subject.

Again, this is a cheap and inexpensive way to fill your blog with content – and if you can find good quality PLR content it is a great way to do things. But I wouldn't recommend using PLR content 'as is.' I'm a huge fan of PLR content – but only as a basis for blog posts. What you want to do is find some good quality PLR content and then re-write it a little. Add bits, take bits away, re-write certain sentences. Doing this will put your stamp on the content and it will make it unique to you.

If you use PLR content 'as is' this will generally get penalized by the search engines. Not only that but it makes your content less valuable. People will come to your blog because they want to read what YOU have got to say and

YOUR content. Use PLR content. I'm a huge fan of it – but do make sure that you make it unique to yourself. It's not hard and the results are well worth it.

Create Unique Content

The ultimate kind of content is that which is unique to your blog. As we have already discussed, people will come to your blog because they want to read your content and your blog posts. If you want new, unique content then you have two main options: You can either write your blog posts yourself or you can outsource them to someone else.

Outsourcing

This is a good option (especially for niche blogs) but it incurs a cost, whereas if you're writing the posts yourself it isn't going to cost you anything to run your blog. If you want to outsource your blog posts then the key is to find a good writer. There's little point in outsourcing your blog posts to a cheap writer, only to find that their writing is so poor you then must spend hours re-writing everything.

So where can you find writers? There are lots of websites for this. You can either browse through their profiles and contact them – or you can post your job on there and let suitable workers apply to you.

Finding a good writer is only half the battle. The key to getting back the content you want is to accurately and thoroughly brief the writer so that they know exactly what you want. Show them the writing style you are looking for. Give them decent article titles and keywords to work from. Point them towards similar blog posts on the internet which they can use as a basis for their writing.

Always remember that your outsourced worker isn't a mind reader. You must show them exactly what you want, otherwise, you'll probably get back something entirely different.

Writing blog posts yourself

If you are writing a personal blog or funds are tight, you will want to write your blog posts yourself. Ultimately these are probably the best kind of blog posts. The content comes from you, and you can bring your blog alive with personal anecdotes and real-life examples.

Coming up with ideas for blog posts

Half the battle is coming up with ideas. You need to ask yourself what people in your niche want to know. If you're not sure, it's very easy to find out. Internet forums are an excellent source of ideas. Have a look at the main topics which people are talking about in your niche and look at the questions people are asking.

Magazines are also an excellent source of ideas. Never copy but look at magazines in your niche and look at the sort of topics they are talking about. A lot of being a blogger is about keeping your eyes open. I often get ideas for blog posts completely randomly – for example, something happens during the day, or I see something and think "that would make a great blog post."

It's a good idea to record your ideas somehow because you just never know when they are going to crop up. I often dictate things or make notes on my iPhone and then look at them again a few days later. A good old-fashioned notebook would do the same job too!

Another place to look is other blogs in your niche. Again, the idea here isn't to copy but to look at their posts as a source of ideas and research. How do you know if a particular topic is popular? Just look at how many comments the post gets. If it gets a lot of comments, then it struck a chord with the readers of that blog – and if your target audience for your blog is the same (or similar) then you would probably write your post on the same subject.

Writing your post

You might be thinking "I can't write" – but trust me, you can! You don't have to be JK Rowling to write a blog. Yes, your blog posts must be fairly well written, but you don't have to be a novelist. The best piece of advice I can give is to write as you speak. Look at most blogs and you'll find that they are written in a fairly simple way. This makes it easier to write and your audience will probably enjoy reading it more.

Let's face it, people don't enjoy reading things which are overly technical and boring. People will come to your blog because they want to find something out, but they *also* want to be entertained at the same time. Have a look at other people's blogs and get a feel for how they are written. I find that this helps a lot and it's a great source of ideas too.

Some tips:

1. Keep it simple. As I say, people don't like reading overly technical things. Keep your language simple and don't use 10 words if 1 will do!

2. Make sure the content is good. At the end of the day, your posts need to contain some good content. There must be a 'main' point for people to get from reading the posts. Try to keep to the subject and don't try to cram too much information into one post.

3. Use stories and examples. As I say, people will read your blog to be informed – but they also want to be entertained too. Adding real-life examples and stories brings your posts alive.

4. Talk about your disasters! A little tip here – people relate to failure and things going wrong, so people LOVE your disaster stories. It also helps to make you seem more 'real' and 'human' – because nobody gets things right 100% of the time.

5. Put your best information first. People generally have a short attention span so it's very important to capture people's attention in the first couple of paragraphs of the post. So – put some of your best information first. Don't hang around and ramble – briefly introduce your post and then launch straight into the main 'meat' of the content.

6. Capture people's attention with your title. The title of the post is very important because it's what draws people in and makes them want to read what you've got to say. I tend to find that slightly unusual and 'different' titles work best – but this will depend on the subject and nature of your blog.

7. Have a clear structure – a beginning, middle and end – the introduction, meat of the content and a conclusion.

8. Format your post. Large chunks of text with no breaks makes your posts hard to read. Make sure you break up your text by keeping your paragraphs short, adding in sub-headings and try putting important words in bold.

9. Also make sure to include keywords in your posts, 'tag' them with relevant keywords and categorize your blog so that people can more easily find the posts they are looking for.

CHAPTER FIVE

Monetizing Your Blog

You'll want to get your blog making you some money. This might be your only reason for blogging – or it might be just one of many. Either way, it's easy to get your blog generating some cash, and we're going to discuss some ways now.

Review Posts

One of my favourite ways of monetizing a blog is to write review posts. You simply review a particular product and then at the end of it you put a link so that people can go ahead and purchase it. This link will be your affiliate link, so you will get paid a commission if someone buys through your link.

The beauty of review posts is that they will get picked up by the search engines when people are searching for the product name. Just make sure that you include the product name a few times during the review.

So how do you write a review post? It doesn't have to be anything fancy. Simply draw up a list of pros and cons about the product in question and then write it up as a review. Try to include some detail about the product – e.g., if it's an eBook, you might want to discuss some of the things the eBook talks about within its content. Make sure to include both positive and negative points in your review and make it 100% honest.

Only write a positive review if you DO like the product. Falsely positively reviewing a product might make you some upfront affiliate commissions but it will serve to earn you a poor reputation. If you recommend rubbish, then people will probably never buy from you again.

So, write a genuine review – and make sure you include some negative points in there too. No matter how much you genuinely like and recommend a product, it will never be perfect and there will always be bits of the product which could be improved. By talking about these things within your review you will find that you will make more sales. People want to hear about the negatives, and it makes your review more believable. A review that is 100% positive screams of "I'm just writing this so people will buy it." If the negatives aren't too serious, it won't put anyone off.

Finally, make sure you draw a conclusion and then subtly point people to the link they should click on if they want to find out more information about it.

Banner Ads

Look at most blogs and you'll see banner adverts dotted around them. These could be links to your products or other people's products you are recommending as an affiliate. You can also sign up for Google AdSense and display ads on your sites that way. When someone clicks on the ads, you get paid a small amount.

Create Your Information Products

If you can write a blog, you can write an information product. It's as simple as that. People come to your blog to tap into your knowledge and expertise – and some of them will be willing to pay for it. Your information product could be an eBook, audio course, video course etc. Whichever you choose, the readers of your blog will make ideal customers.

Turn your blog into a membership site

This is an increasingly common business model. People can read the general posts on your blog for free – but if they want to get access to your "premium" blog content they must pay you a membership fee. This is a model that works and has been used successfully by leading internet marketers such as Lee McIntyre.

It works because the free stuff draws people in and makes them interested in your blog. They can see that you provide a good level of content, and they start to visit your blog regularly to read your content. Many of them will then want to access your higher-level content. This will be additional content and/or exploring in greater depth the things you are talking about on your free blog posts. I like this model and it's something I'm looking to try out at some point.

Sell Ad Space

If you can get to the point where your blog becomes popular and is getting a good amount of traffic, then you could sell advertising space to other marketers. For a fee, people could place banner ads in your sidebar or at the bottom of your posts. Another option is to let people write guest posts where they can advertise their products within the post.

Build a List

Blogs are a great way of building a list – and once you have your list it's possible to make a lot of money online. Quite simply, an email list of subscribers is one of the most important parts of any online business. A list allows you to make money on tap – and even in your sleep. Well, the good news is that your blog is a great way of attracting new subscribers.

Place an opt-in box in a prominent position on your blog and you will find that a decent proportion of your readers will subscribe. Once they have done so you can then send them email promotions (your products and affiliate products) as well as notify them of when you make new posts on your blog.

This links in very well with review posts. You can send out an email to your subscribers promoting a product as an affiliate – but instead of sending them directly to the offer page you simply link them to your review on your blog. If they are interested in it, they can then click on your link at the end of the review and buy it. My testing shows that this usually increases conversions.

You can see an example of an opt-in box on a blog in the screenshot below:

Flip Your Blog

There is a lot of money to be made by creating and then selling blogs. This is known as 'flipping' – and if your blog is well established you can generate a lot of income in this way. You can use sites such as Flippa (http://www.flippa.com) to advertise your blog to prospective purchasers. 'Sounds good – but how much could I expect to make from selling my blog?' That's a hard question to answer but in my experience, the value of a blog is determined by three main things.

1. How much traffic the blog receives every month
2. How well established the blog is
3. How much money does the blog earn

The more money the blog earns and the more traffic it receives every month, the more it will be worth. Blogs that are well established, have a high readership level and which earn money consistently are very valuable indeed and can sell for $1000s, depending on how much exactly the blog earns.

Other factors also come into play, for example, the niche, the design of the blog, the quality of the domain name and the quality of the content – but ultimately the value usually boils down to traffic and income.

So, there is a lot of money to be made by establishing a niche blog, developing it and monetizing it for a year or two – and then selling it. You can of course establish a brand-new blog and sell it straight away. It will have some value but realistically this isn't going to be very much.

CHAPTER SIX

Driving Traffic to Your Blog

All blogs need traffic. Without it your blog is pointless, to say the least – but how do you generate traffic? Well, it isn't that hard, but it does require some work. As your blog becomes more established, you should find that people start to come back to your blog again and again. Your blog posts will get picked up by the search engines too (they love blogs) but in the early days especially you're probably going to have to invest quite a bit of effort in traffic generation.

So, I'm going to take you through some of my favourite methods that you can use to get yourself started.

1. Blog commenting

One of the best ways of driving some traffic is by using other people's blogs. The beauty of using blog commenting as a traffic method is that you can easily attract exactly the target audience whom you want to visit your blog – and best of all is that it is completely free. So, to get started, you, first need to find other related blogs in your niche.

You might already know them – but even if you don't (or you want to find new ones) a quick Google search for keywords related to your niche + the word 'blog' should uncover some good ones. You want to look for blogs that receive a high amount of traffic themselves. There is little point in spending hours commenting on blogs if nobody is ever going to see your comments... How do you know if a blog gets a lot of traffic?

Just look at the number of comments the posts get. If a blog is regularly getting at least 10 comments, then you can usually be confident that it receives a decent amount of traffic and thus is worth our time and attention. Find some related blogs which look like they fit the bill and then go and make some comments.

Within the form, you fill in to leave your comment there should be a field where you can enter a web address. Here you want to enter your blog web address. People will see your comments and (hopefully) click on your link and check out your blog. What you want to do is leave insightful comments containing some good information. Never just say "great post" and leave that as your comment. Doing this makes it obvious that you are just spamming in the hope of generating some traffic.

You want to leave detailed comments. It's fine to say "great post" so long as you say why you enjoyed it. If you can, show your knowledge and prove to people that you are an expert on this subject. If you can appear like an expert, people will check out your blog too.

Try to add to the conversation. Maybe pick a couple of points out of the original post and add your thoughts/opinions on it. Raise new questions and challenge what the post is saying if you don't 100% agree with it. Always look for ways of demonstrating your knowledge. This is the secret to successfully using blog commenting as a traffic generation method – and trust me, if you do it right it IS highly effective. You also of course get backlinks back to your blog, which is good for SEO and can help your blog to rank higher in the search engines.

2. Article marketing

Article marketing is one of the most well-known traffic generation methods, but it is still very effective. Write good solid articles and submit them to article directories. Contact other blog owners and ask if you can submit one of your articles as a guest post. On a similar note, contact content site owners and submit your articles to them too. At the end of your article, simply link back to your blog or a specific post.

3. Viral marketing

Viral marketing is a very underused and underrated method. You don't see many people talking about viral marketing, yet it is a very effective way of getting free traffic in your online business. Create a good quality eBook with solid content and include links inside to your blog. Distribute it to as many people as you can and encourage them to pass it on. Give it away or send it to eBay sellers, etc.

4. Traffic from your list

Once you have built a list it is very easy to drive an instant surge of people to your blog simply by telling your subscribers whenever you make a new post.

Conclusion

Blogging is a great way to make money online. Whether you become a niche blogger or a personal blogger, it can be both great fun and extremely profitable.

So, what are the keys to running a successful blog? At the heart of it is great content. You want people to come back to your blog again and again and become regular readers. If you can do that, you will begin to build up a relationship with your readers and they are then more likely to buy your products and services.

Blogs are great for relationship building. They provide the ideal platform to share your knowledge, experience, and tips – and allow people to respond and add their comments to the conversation.

I hope that you found this guide useful and that it will aid you in setting up your blog. Blogging isn't rocket science – but it does require thoughtful effort using some of the techniques and ideas we have discussed in this report.

I wish you the very best of luck.

9 798885 214131

Printed by Libri Plureos GmbH in Hamburg, Germany